SIMONE'S PLACE

SIMONE'S PLACE

A Play

by

Glenville Lovell

CHATTEL HOUSE BOOKS

ISBN 978-0-9848033-3-0

Dedicated to all those involved in the struggle for the rights of LGBT people all over the world.

INTRODUCTION

One sunny day in May of 2012, I sat down with a project coordinator of a Government Agency in Barbados to discuss a project dealing with issues affecting the LGBT community in that country. The project coordinator cited the rising cases of abandonment, rejection and ostracism against the lesbian, gay, bisexual and transgender community in Barbados, and wanted to do something to highlight the need for Barbadians to reassess their attitudes and behaviours towards the LGBT community.

The drawn subject, while quite timely and important, was also a controversial one even in Barbados' somewhat passive-aggressive social milieu, but I was moved by the coordinator's passion and agreed without reservation to put all my creative energy into constructing the imaginary world needed to explore this subject though I knew, going in, that my invention might present a significant challenge to the sensibilities of some in Barbados.

It did not take me long to devise an approach to the play, and I did not have to look very far for characters either. The short story, *Court Jesters*, in my published collection, *Going Home in Chains,* provided me with both. Most of the characters in *Simone's Place* jumped willingly from the pages of *Court Jesters* into the cabaret shelter that is the setting for this play, bringing with them the same charged sexuality, raw human emotion and humor. The addition of music was the final touch.

The first draft of the play took about 3 months to finish. My trusted friend, Icil Philips, read it and provided worthy feedback and clear critical analysis. The director, Russell Watson, also contributed a valuable critical eye on subsequent drafts and his ability to pull fragmented scenes together helped to focus the dramatic action. In November of 2012, I flew to Barbados to attend the first public reading of the play. It would take another year and a half before we finally got Simone's Place into rehearsal, but in May 2014, we held up the shiny mirror for a Barbadian audience. Time will tell if they liked what they saw.

Glenville Lovell

A NOTE ON MUSIC

Quite a bit of music was used in the original production. Most of it were songs sung by Nina Simone during her wonderful career. However, the songs used in the finale came out of a genre of Barbadian music called Spouge. One of those songs was originally done by Toots and the Maytals, and then covered by the Barbadian duo, The Draytons. The other song was recorded by The Lunar 7, a popular Spouge group of the seventies in Barbados.

SIMONE'S PLACE *was first presented at Frank Collymore Hall in Barbados on May 9, 2014, produced by Marlene Hewitt and Merle Niles, with the following cast:*

LADY SIMONE	SHANNON ARTHUR
MOSES	NALA
PECONG	SIMON ALLEYNE
STUART	MARCUS MYERS
GABRIEL	JOHN HUNTE
SOLACE	VARIA WILLIAMS

Dancers:
Kendra Grazette, Jalessa Daisley, Lisa Davis

Directed by Russell Watson
Scene Design by Leandro Soto
Costumes by Russell Watson
Choreography by Shakeira Beckles
Produced by Marlene Hewitt & Merle Niles

.

ALSO BY GLENVILLE LOVELL

NOVELS:
Fire in the Canes
Song of Night
Too Beautiful to Die
Love and Death in Brooklyn
The Darkest Street

STORIES:
Going Home in Chains

PLAYS:
On the Block
Panama Silver

SIMONE'S PLACE

PROLOGUE

*Black. In silhouette, a woman stands upstage with her back to the audience on a platform. Soft spotlight on woman as we hear the opening bars of **Nina Simone's I Put a Spell** on You. Transgender,* LADY SIMONE, *in a clinging red dress, turns to face to the audience. The spotlight opens out as she descends the platform and moves downstage.*

SIMONE   Ladies and Gentlemen, welcome to Simone's Place. A cabaret like no other on this island. And that, I'm sure, is why you're here. You've heard that in Simone's Place, magic is real. Transformations take place before your eyes. We give you music and dance that has the power to heal broken hearts and to stir passions that last lifetimes. We only ask one thing. Open your minds and your hearts, for only then can we truly share in the transformative union of souls. I am Lady Simone, the owner of this establishment. Some call me the Queen of Passion, some have called me worse. But tonight, I'm just a woman trying to cast a spell on you... and you... and you. (*She laughs and begins to sing* I Put a Spell on You.) (*Blackout.*)

ACT ONE

SCENE ONE

Early evening. Lights come up in Simone's Place to the voice of Nina Simone singing Times They Are A Changin. *The open-air club/bar is attached to Lady Simone's private residence. Corrugated iron walls, the floor, the tables and chairs/stools are colorfully painted in combinations of yellow, green, blue, red; reflecting the sensibility of the Santeria Orisha Oya. A bar in one corner. Door off to the right leads to a storeroom. Wearing a fitted shirt, Stuart, the bartender, is storing drinks in the cooler beneath the bar. Moses enters. There is a wild, yet controlled quality to Moses' bearing. In his hand is an object wrapped in newsprint.*

STUART   Hey Moses.

MOSES   Wuh wukkin', Stuart?

STUART   Only me. And hard.

MOSES   Where Simone?

STUART   Snoring. Show was kinda flat last night. You know how she gets when that happens.

MOSES   Yeah, depressed. And drunk.

STUART   You know your, girl. She's still sleeping it off. I've been trying to tell her the show needs a makeover. Adapted a bit. But she's stubborn.

MOSES   You open yet?

STUART   You know we always open for you.

MOSES   Gimme a beer.

STUART   (*Serves beer.*) Where you off to?

MOSES   Martinique.

STUART   A show?

MOSES   Yeah. And in a few weeks the biennial in Cuba.

STUART   You always on the go, man.

MOSES   I en got no degree, boy, so I gotta push. Gotta hustle. Good thing I like to travel.

STUART   I going New York in a few days.

MOSES   Vacation?

STUART   Funeral. My uncle.

MOSES   Sorry to hear... Wunna did close?

STUART   Very. He taught me to play the piano. Used to take me to Broadway shows whenever I went to New York. Gonna miss him a lot.

MOSES   You got anybody else in New York?

STUART   My mother. And a sister. I got my green card, too. Could stay if I want.

MOSES   Why don't you?

STUART   Been thinking about it.

MOSES   This place dead as Vaucluse plantation, son. Educated man like you shouldn't be working no bar. Go and make your name, dread.

STUART   May stay six months this time, see if I like it.

MOSES   (*Puts object in his hand on bar.*) This for Simone. She asked me to make it for a friend of hers.

STUART   Want me to get her?

MOSES   Naw, let her get her beauty sleep. (STUART *laughs.*) I hear you telling somebody the other day that you come from Belleplaine.

STUART   Yeah. Came up here to live with my father after my mother went away.

MOSES   I used to know a man from Belleplaine.

STUART   I would think you know a lot of people from Belleplaine.

MOSES   Yes... But this man... He was different. You remind me of him.

STUART   How so? You mean I look like him?

MOSES   (*Getting up. Puts 5 dollars on bar.*) He... He was a nice guy. Like you. (*Starts off.*) Well, I'm off

STUART   Moses. (MOSES *stops. Turns.*) Never mind. (MOSES *exits.* STUART *returns to his task as lights fade on Nina Simone's* Times They Are A Changin.)

ACT ONE

SCENE TWO

Late evening. Simone's Place. SIMONE, *dressed for rehearsal in white sweats, with her head wrapped in a white cloth, Orisha beads hang from her neck, hums as she fiddles with the controls on a boom-box sitting on the bar.* SIMONE *turns from the boom-box and the beginning chords of a Nina* SIMONE *standard spill out. The song is:* I Wish I Knew How It Would Feel To Be Free. *Her phone rings. She turns boom-box off and hunts her cell phone which is in her bag on a chair somewhere.*

SIMONE   Hello... Lottie, don't tell me no foolishness... I'm trying to rehearse here, okay. I don't need to hear this nonsense. Those costumes need to be ready by next week... I don't care... Woman, do you know who you're messing with?... Not my problem. You should've thought of it before you took the job. Find the material. Fly to China if you have to. But get me my damn costumes here by next Friday. (SIMONE *turns music on. She begins her rehearsal. She stops from time to time to count out dance steps or rephrase a particular bit of music, or change a dance step. After a few more times she stops in frustration. Curses. Turns the music off. She opens her bag and takes a bottle of pills. Goes behind counter and pours a glass of water.* STUART *enters.*)

STUART   Hi Simone.

SIMONE   Stuart? What you doing here? Aren't you leaving for New York today?

STUART   Yeah, but I need to talk to you about something. I need your advice.

SIMONE   Give me a minute, honey. Gotta take my pills. (*Takes pills from bottle. Swallows with water.* STUART *takes 2 chairs from stack. He sits.* SIMONE *puts pills back into her bag. Opens beer.*)

STUART   Hormones?

SIMONE   Big enough to choke a horse. Want a drink?

STUART   No, I good.

SIMONE   Have a beer. You look stressed.

STUART   I good. I good.

SIMONE   (*Approaches* STUART *with beer in her hand. Sits. Takes long sip.*) Aaah! Nothing like a good beer after aggravation. You don't like beer, do you?

STUART   No. Not much.

SIMONE   Why not?

STUART   I don't know. I've always preferred champagne.

SIMONE   Yeah, I forgot you hot shots love to ball like that.

STUART   I had another visitation last night.

SIMONE   Your uncle?

STUART   Wearing red and black.

SIMONE   Legba, I give thanks. (*Makes sign of cross.*)

STUART   How old were you when you came out?

SIMONE   When I did what... You mean?

STUART   Yeah.

SIMONE   I was never in, honey. I was always a woman. This dangling participle between my legs will be edited out very soon. I feel like a man born with a tail.

STUART   Yesterday my wutless uncle tried to fix me up with one of his old girlfriends. Woman nearly old enough to be my mother. Told him since I stopped nursing I'm allergic to udders, but he didn't get the joke.

SIMONE   Seriously, Stu? Udders? (*They laugh.*) Tell me. How's the Phantom?

STUART   Don't call him that.

SIMONE   Either that or Invisible Man. Take your pick. At least until I see his face.

STUART   My mother's going to try to get me to stay in New York.

SIMONE   And you're thinking…

STUART   Do I have reason enough to come back?

SIMONE   Look, Stu. Make sure you know what you're doing. Don't get so bewitch behind this man that you can't see your future.

STUART   Like how you bewitch behind Moses?

SIMONE   (*Laughs. Pushes* STUART *playfully.*) You need to mind your business.

STUART   I don't know, Simone. Moses… I don't know. Moses is an enigma. Something interesting happened the other day. Before he left for Martinique. He was telling me about a man he knew in Belleplaine and I got this strange feeling as he was talking.

SIMONE   What kind of feeling?

STUART   I don't know. That we're connected somehow. Me and him and this man.

SIMONE   Maybe you are. Guess what? I got a reading done last week. She told me my soul mate is closer than I think.

STUART   But is it Moses?

SIMONE   Who knows? Sometimes I feel I'm destined to be alone for the rest of my days.

STUART   You have the club.

SIMONE   I have the club? What kind of shite talk is that? You don't think I deserve to have somebody love me the way you say the Phantom loves you?

STUART   I didn't mean...

SIMONE   I know what you mean. All you see is the costume and the makeup. The glitz and the laughter. You don't see beneath that.

STUART   No, Simone. I have so much respect for you. You're an amazing, strong woman. And you do amazing things. The work you do with UGLAAB is amazing.

SIMONE   Blah! Blah! Blah! I'm amazing. I'm amazing. I'm also lonely. Even the strongest tree needs rain.

STUART   I didn't mean it that way. (*Long pause.*) How should I tell my father?

SIMONE   Think carefully about what you expect to happen. Your father is from another planet. And it en one that anywhere close to the earth either.

STUART   You're right. He's not very happy with me as it is. He destroyed my altar and the offerings I had for Elegba. On Monday, I had put some strong black coffee, a glass of rum, some fresh fruit and a Cuban cigar on the altar. He went into my room and threw them out, along with the candles and everything else. Tell me I practicing Obeah.

SIMONE   You lucky he didn't call the police.

STUART I have to tell him.

SIMONE You don't think he already knows or suspects?

STUART I'm sure he hears the rumors. But I need to do it. To stand in front of him and say it.

SIMONE I understand. You need to sing inside your story. I don't know what I would do if I was in your shoes. I didn't have a choice really. From the time I was four I knew I was different. Lucky for me, I had an aunt who understood. Like she knew that I was supposed to be a girl. Bought me my first dress at six. Introduced me Nina Simone's music when I was ten. The rest, as they say, is history. Did I tell you about the time I met her in Paris?

STUART Who? Nina?

SIMONE Yes. Was nineteen ninety-five or six. I flew all the way there to hear her. She was magical as I expected. A friend of mine knew her manager, so I got to meet her afterwards. She wore this simple black dress. Looked beautiful on her. She looked tired and slurred a bit when she talked, but her eyes were still fierce. When I told her I was from Barbados, her face lit up. It made me feel so special. Then I ruined it.

STUART How?

SIMONE I told her my father had been a good friend of Errol Barrow's. Her eyes slashed me from the top of my head to my chin. Then she lit a cigarette and blew smoke in my eyes. I was dismissed. But, like a true groupie, I loved her even more for that moment of abuse.

STUART (*Laughs*) You're crazy. I gotta go get ready.

SIMONE (*They hug.* STUART *starts off.*) Stuart? (STUART *turns.*) You were right. The show is getting stale. What can I do give it some... You know?

STUART   Hmmm... I don't know. Ask Solace. She's always full of ideas.

SIMONE   Please God! No. Not Solace. That mad woman would have me stripping in the club. *(Pause.)* That visitation. Your uncle. He's telling you his soul is at peace now.

STUART   I hope so.

SIMONE   Have a safe flight. (STUART *exits. Lights fade as* SIMONE *leaves stage humming.*)

ACT ONE

SCENE THREE

A month later. Evening. Sun setting on Simone's Place. MOSES *and* SIMONE *standing near the bar in conversation. Simone is dressed in white pants and rainbow patterned blouse. She's got a colored band around her head and she's also wearing her Orisha bead bracelets representing Oya. We hear Nina Simone's* I want Some Sugar in My Bowl *rising softly. Moses is dressed in shorts and T-shirt. His friend,* PECONG, *a thick, stocky man, wearing jeans, a red baseball cap and sneakers, enters.* PECONG *begins to unstack the chairs.*

PECONG   Moses, is something I gotta talk to you 'bout, man.

MOSES   If it's money, I broke.

SIMONE   (*Noticing* PECONG *unstacking chairs.*) What're you doing?

PECONG   Wuh you mean what I doing? You en see I getting a chair to sit down?

SIMONE   We en open yet.

PECONG   Wuh you mean, you en open? Moses drinking.

SIMONE   Moses is here in private conversation with me. Come back in an hour.

PECONG   I en stopping wunna from privately conversating.

MOSES   Wuh you need to talk to me 'bout, Pecong?

PECONG   Don't leh me stop you from conversating, man. It could wait. That bitch like she waan bite off my head. Like if I interested in wunna conversation.

SOLACE   (*Entering with a cigarette in her mouth. She's dressed in tight shorts and very revealing top and flip flops.*) Moses, just the man I was looking for.

MOSES   Wuh gine on, Solace? I just pass and shout you.

SOLACE   Shout fuh me wuh! You en shout fuh me one rass. I was in my bed schlicking, so I know you en shout me. Hearing you voice woulda make me cum hard as shite.

SIMONE   (*Laughing.*) Solace, girl, you en easy at all.

SOLACE   Somebody tell me you was back in the land. Say you bring back a Cuban woman.

MOSES   Where you hear that?

SOLACE   A little birdie.

PECONG   Lemme guess where that birdie was. Up in you?

SOLACE   Well it wasn't yours. And never will be. So, you could keep on fantasizing.

PECONG   Mine? To let it drop off.

SOLACE   From what I hear it ready to drop off all like now.

SIMONE   Alright. It too early fuh the two ah wunna to start wunna shtupidness.

SOLACE   Simone, bring a flask fuh me, girl.

PECONG   So how come you en tell she you close?

SOLACE   You close?

SIMONE   Just opened. But I en giving you nuh more credit, you know, Solace

SOLACE   Girl, I got a job. I don't need credit. In fact, I buying for everybody

PECONG   (*Mocking laugh.*) You got a job? Doing wuh?

SOLACE   Everybody except Pecong, that is. I working for Moses, if you must know. Jipsee wretch.

PECONG   Wuh Moses en got nuh pig pen to clean out.

MOSES   Pecong, man.

SOLACE   You leave he, Moses. You leave he to the Lord. Wuh you drinking?

MOSES   Banks.

PECONG   Man, Moses, if you done conversating I really gotta talk to you.

MOSES   You en just say it could wait? (*Simone puts a beer, a flask and a shot glass on the counter.* MOSES *picks up beer.* SIMONE *puts flask and shot glass on tray and takes to* SOLACE.)

PECONG   It look like you done conversating so come let we…

SOLACE   Wait, you think I going to buy he a drink and leh he go long so?

MOSES   Have a drink and relax for a minute, man.

PECONG   You en hear the woman say, she en buying for me.

MOSES   Wuh you drinking?

PECONG   A warm Guinness.

SIMONE   Five dollars.

PECONG   Moses?

SIMONE   Awright then.

MOSES   (*Puts 5 dollars on bar.*) You hear the man. A Guinness fuh the gentleman in the red hat. (SIMONE *opens Guinness.* PECONG *walks over to fetch it.*)

SOLACE   Moses, I saw your picture in the paper the other day.

MOSES   I en see it, but I hear so.

SOLACE   Picture of you by the waterfall down by Bath.

MOSES   Oh, must be the one Simone take for the newsletter.

SOLACE   Hmmm... You and Simone went down by Bath taking pictures. I bet yuh won't go down there with me.

SIMONE   I forgot to tell you, Moses. One of the newspapers picked up the story I wrote in Going Pottery about your trip to Martinique. And talking 'bout that. I want to interview you for the next issue about your trip to Cuba. Did you get to meet Castro?

MOSES   Wanted to, but he wasn't well.

PECONG   You lucky them communist let you leave.

SOLACE   Pecong, why you always gotta display your ignorance for everybody to see? Simone, you does interview Moses every week. How about interviewing me for a change. I got interesting things to say, too, yuh know.

SIMONE   It's a newsletter about potters, Solace. Not people with a potty mouth.

SOLACE   We could talk about my new job?

SIMONE   Which is?

SOLACE   Don't let Pecong know, but I helping Albert in his shop. So that makes me a potter's assistant.

PECONG   Don't let Pecong know? What, I right here. I can hear you.

SOLACE   Or you can write about how I raising three children without a man.

SIMONE   That's half the women in Barbados, Solace.

SOLACE   But half ain't get abandoned by their family at fifteen because they was pregnant, and still went on and to finish high school while living in a cardbox in a neighbor's backyard?

PECONG   You believe she with that story?

SOLACE   Pecong, who ask you?

MOSES   Pecong, come leh me hear what it is you got to tell me. (MOSES *starts off.*)

SIMONE   Moses, don't go 'long home, yuh know. I really want to do that interview today.

MOSES   I coming back. (MOSES *exits with* PECONG.)

SOLACE   Simone, I hear you looking for new ideas for the show. What you should do is mix in some spouge. People getting tired seeing you do them same drug addict songs over and over.

SIMONE   Nina Simone was no drug addict.

SOLACE   All them black American blues singers is drug addicts. Yuh would have to be a druggie or depressed to be singing that shite every night.

SIMONE   (*Laughing.*) Solace, leave my place.

SOLACE   Tell me the truth. You don't feel like breaking open a flask after singing one a them songs? Shite, man. Depressing. (*Sings mockingly.*)
I put a spell on you

'cause you're mine
You better stop the things you do
I ain't lyin' (*Stops singing. Laughs.*)
Begging a man to stop cheating is like asking the river to stop
flowing. (*Sings.*)
I pour some piss on you
'cause you're worthless
And I hope you never breathe again.
And I ent lying
(*Finishes singing.*)
Now, that's what them words to the song should be.

SIMONE   Solace, you drunk.

SOLACE   Now, wuh you should be singing is spouge. In fact, I
think you should change your name from Lady Simone to
Madame Spouge. I believe spouge is ready to make a come-
back.

SIMONE   Nina Simone singing spouge. You must be crazy.

SOLACE   What so crazy 'bout that? From what I hear the Dipper
put nuff spouge up in she backside when she was living here.
Even in the canes. Had she whistling like cane blades in the
wind. A kinda blues-spouge mix would sound good.(*Laughs.*)

SIMONE   This is the thanks I get for letting you drink in my establishment? What you know 'bout spouge anyway? That was
before you time.

SOLACE   Can I ask you something seriously, though?

SIMONE   What, sugar?

SOLACE   What would you do… Suppose you met this man…
You's a woman with children and you met this man… You's
a woman that had it rough. I mean rough.

SIMONE   We talking 'bout you?

SOLACE   Hear me out, nuh.

SIMONE   Go 'head.

SOLACE   You don't trust men 'cause every one you had... they try
to rule you. To control you. So you meet a man... He en from
'bout here.

SIMONE   Meaning?

SOLACE   He en Bajan. But he seems... He seems nice enough.
And he got money. He wants to marry you. To take care of
you and your children. But there is this other man who you
can't seem to get off you mind. He... You feel like if you could
just get him to see you... Really see you inside... know you...
But he seem... He don't really want to look. What should I
do?

SIMONE   So we talking about you?

SOLACE   What should I do?

SIMONE   Do you love this man?

SOLACE   Which one?

SIMONE   The one you can't get off you mind.

SOLACE   I think so. One time we get drunk... at his house. And
we end up in bed. Nothing happened. But that's what's so special about him. Most men I know woulda take advantage of
the situation. But not he. He en that sorta person.

SIMONE   He knows how you feel?

SOLACE   I give him hints but he just act like it's all a joke.

SIMONE   Stop giving hints. Tell him how you feel.

SOLACE   Is that what you would do?

SIMONE   Yes.

SOLACE   So, you told Moses?

SIMONE   Me and Moses... That's different.

SOLACE   Because you know you en got what he wants.

SIMONE   Who say... Who say I en got what he wants?

SOLACE   I say so.
(GABRIEL *enters. He has the appearance of a man who is care-ful about his looks and the way he dresses. He stands looking around.*)

SIMONE   You come to drink or sight-see?

GABRIEL   I'm sorry. I was just... I'm Gabriel. You must be Lady Simone.

SIMONE   (*With flourish.*) Did I just hear my cue? (*Sings a few bars of* I Put a Spell on You.)

GABRIEL   (*Applauds.*) I've heard a lot about you. And now I can see why Stu lights up when he talks about you.

SOLACE   And I'm Solace. (*Extends hand.* GABRIEL *shakes her hand.*) You musta hear a lot 'bout me, too. I'm by far the most interesting person up here.

GABRIEL   Solace?

SOLACE   Lady Solace, if you prefer.

GABRIEL   What interesting things would I've heard about you?

SIMONE   Don't get her started. Solace, why you don't go 'long home and look after them girls?

SOLACE   I should go make sure Dinah done she homework. (*Finishes her drink, puts the cork on the flask.*) We'll pick this up later, Gabe. You don't mind if I call you Gabe, right? (*laughs and leaves.*)

SIMONE   If you're looking for Stu, he isn't here.

GABRIEL   I... Yes. I...

SIMONE   You want a drink?

GABRIEL   Ah... no. I was... Do you know if he's home?

SIMONE   You know where he lives.

GABRIEL   No... Yes, but I prefer...

SIMONE   He's not here. That's all I can tell you.

GABRIEL   Do you know if he's back from New York?

SIMONE   If Stuart wanted you to know if he was back, I'm sure he would've told you. (*There is an awkward silence as* GABRIEL *realizes he will get no information from* SIMONE. PECONG *and* MOSES *enter.* GABRIEL *turns to leave.* PECONG *is in his way and refuses to move.* GABRIEL *awkwardly sidesteps* PECONG *and leaves.*)

PECONG   Who's that?

SIMONE   Where?

PECONG   That just left.

SIMONE   Why didn't you ask him?

PECONG   Your boyfriend?

SIMONE   What if it was?

PECONG   Tired of all these stinking bullers, man. I gine stop coming in this club.

SIMONE   What is that you just say?

PECONG   I say I tired of all wunna stinking bullers, man. Tired. Got the place confuse, ah.

SIMONE   The only body in here confused is you, Pecong.

MOSES   Pecong, why you don't shut up, nuh man? Come and have a drink. Simone, bring a flask and two glasses.

PECONG   And why you always taking up fuh them?

MOSES   If you don't like Simone's place why you always in here?

PECONG   You en hear me say I going to stop? You think I don't see the two ah wunna whispering all the time. And I see how she does be looking at you.

SIMONE   (*Putting flask and glasses on table.* MOSES *pours into both glasses.*) What? You jealous?

PECONG   All wunna bullers so want killing.

SIMONE   Moses, you better car' he 'long from in here before I forget how I was raised and start acting like a twenty dollar whore. I won't want you to see that side of me.

MOSES   Come and have a drink, man. (*Puts arm around* PECONG *to calm him down.*)

PECONG   (*Disengages.*) Don't touch me, man.

MOSES   Come Pecong, man.

PECONG   (*Pushes* MOSES *away forcefully, and takes pugnacious stance.*) Ah say don't touch me.

MOSES   What? You waan fight with me now, too? Wuh going on with you, man? You en acting right. Ever since you leave you child mother, you getting on prickly.

SIMONE   Prickly is the right word.

MOSES   If you miss the woman, go and get she back. Yuh tell me you wanted to talk to me and when we went outside all yuh do is stare at the ground like you's a bloodhound.

SIMONE   Pecong.

PECONG   Don't call my name, hear!

SIMONE   Whatever it is that bothering you, it don't give you the right to disrespect me. And in my own place at that. Now, I've been very patient.

PECONG   You waan be a patient?

SIMONE   He-he-he… Very funny. Now leave my place before I throw you out.

PECONG   (PECONG *starts off. Turns to* MOSES.) Leh she keep whispering in you ear. (*Exits.*)

MOSES   This en the Pecong I know. I don't understand.

SIMONE   Pecong can piss off for now. We have an interview to do.

MOSES   I en really feeling that now, yuh know.

SIMONE   Shouldn't take long. Let me get my Ipad. (SIMONE *leaves.*)

MOSES   I en see Stuart in a while. He still in New York?

SIMONE   (*Offstage.*) Wuh Stuart want ain't in America.

MOSES   And what is that?

SIMONE   (*Returning with Ipad.*) What is it we all want?

MOSES   Money?

SIMONE   (*Smiles.*) Yes, Moses. (SIMONE *opens a beer and moves to sit across from* MOSES. *She takes a sip and sighs.*) We all want money. But what else? Is that all you want?

MOSES   Me? I just concentrate on work.

SIMONE   And when the work is done... When night falls?

MOSES   The work is never done. We doing the interview or not?

SIMONE   (*Begins recording.*) So, tell me, what were your impressions of Cuba? Did you go to Callejón de Hamel?

MOSES   I did. Amazing place. The murals. The music. Thanks for telling me about it.

SIMONE   I bet you felt the spirit of the Orishas when you were there.

MOSES   I felt the music.

SIMONE   Oh, you felt them. Don't be afraid to admit it.

MOSES   (*Laughs.*) If you say so.

SIMONE   Did you get to see a lot of the country? Meet people?

MOSES   Not as much though as I woulda like... I got to drive through the country a bit. Visit a few schools. Everybody seemed to be involved with something artistic. Music. Dance. Drama. Was exciting to see. The artists there are very focused and well trained.

SIMONE   Did you meet anybody interesting?

MOSES   Interesting?

SIMONE You know… a woman... Women? That you like… You know.

MOSES Not really.

SIMONE So you didn't bring back a girlfriend from Cuba?

MOSES You mind Solace with that talk?

SIMONE Heard she was very pretty. With short black hair. Like a boy's.

MOSES She wasn't my girlfriend.

SIMONE But she came back with you?

MOSES She wasn't my girlfriend.

SIMONE How come you don't have a girlfriend? I never hear you talk 'bout nuh girlfriend.

MOSES What that got to do with pottery?

SIMONE Fans want to know these things. What's in inside your heart.

MOSES I put it all in my work.

SIMONE Don't you plan to settle down? Have children?

MOSES If it happens, it happens.

SIMONE Maybe you looking for something different.

MOSES Like wuh?

SIMONE Like… I don't know. Something different. Love don't always come in a conventional package, yuh know. Not always. Sometimes it comes when you least expect. From someplace you didn't even know it existed.

MOSES   Wuh you getting at?

SIMONE   (*Flustered.*) Just that… I don't know.

MOSES   (*Long pause. Gets up.*) There's something that I don't get.

SIMONE   What?

MOSES   You and Pecong. The two a wunna used to get along real good. You do he something?

SIMONE   Not a thing.

MOSES   You en surprised at the way he behaving?

SIMONE   Moses, if I was to take on every little twist and turn in life, every different face that people show me… If I was to study that I wouldn't be where I is today. I was seeing two-faced people from the time I put on my first dress.

MOSES   Awright then. See yuh.

SIMONE   Moses… You have any old spouge records home?

MOSES   Spouge? No. But I know a fella who used play at dances and thing. He would have some, I believe. You want me to check?

SIMONE   Would you? Thanks.

MOSES   No problem.

SIMONE   (MOSES *leaves.* SIMONE *sits in silence for a while. Then she screams.*) You damn fool!
(*Black.*)

ACT ONE

SCENE FOUR

Late night. A few days later. The club is dark. We hear banging at the door. SIMONE *emerges from her bedroom in nightgown. She turns on lights and then grabs a cutlass from behind the bar. Progresses cautiously to the door and peeps out. Recognizing who's there, she puts the cutlass back and then opens the door.* STUART *stumbles in dragging a suitcase. His face is bruised.*

SIMONE   Oh my God! Stuart? Wuh happen to you? (SIMONE *tries to examine his face.* STUART *shrugs her off and goes to get a drink.* SIMONE *follows him.* STUART *pours himself a drink.* SIMONE *finally gets a chance to see just how badly he is injured.*]) Wuh happen? You get in an accident?

STUART   You want a drink?

SIMONE   No, I don't want a drink. What happened to you? (STUART *downs drink. Leans unsteadily on the counter.*) I'm calling the doctor.

STUART   I'm OK.

SIMONE   Excuse me?

STUART   I said I'm OK.

SIMONE   Am I dreaming, then? Because if I am, then you need to get out of my dream. You're definitely not the man I want in my dreams.

STUART   Family drama.

SIMONE   Oh no.

STUART   Oh yes. (SIMONE *brings icepack.stuart takes icepack from* SIMONE. *Holds it to his face.*) I told my mother when I

was in New York. She told my backward father. He was wait-
ing when I got back. Won't even let me into the house. Cuffed
me in the face. I hit him back so hard...

SIMONE   You did what?

STUART   Knocked his ass to the ground, nuh! And scrammed out
of there.

SIMONE   *(Touches* STUART'S *muscular arm.)* Oh my! Maybe you
are the man of my dreams after all.

STUART   Can I stay here?

SIMONE   Boy, do you work fast. *(Laughs.)* Of course, honey.

STUART   Thanks.

SIMONE   You sure you're OK, though? Any dizziness?

STUART   Nothing that a bottle of your champagne can't cure.

SIMONE   I bet you orchestrated all this so you can get at my
champagne. (SIMONE *brings a bottle of champagne.*) So, guess
who is no longer the Invisible Man. (*They look at each other
and begin to laugh.*)

STUART   Did he really?

SIMONE   Waltzed through my door like he was King Jah Jah.

STUART   I didn't think he knew how to find the place.

SIMONE   *(Playful French accent.)* Ma chéri! What're you talking
about? Everybody knows how to get to Simone's Place.

STUART   Looks like my tactics might be working.

SIMONE   What tactic is that?

STUART   I didn't call him once all the time I was away.

SIMONE Does he know you're back?

STUART Texted him from the airport. He wanted to pick me up, but I told him no. He was so hurt. You should've heard him.

SIMONE Well, I hope you have more luck with your tactic than I had with mine.

STUART What happened? (SIMONE *doesn't respond.*) Oh my God! You told Moses you loved him?

SIMONE Damn close. I came onto him, but he knocked me to the ground. I'm still searching for nose. (STUART *Laughs.*) Stu, it ain't funny. My head's here ready to run away and leave my foolish heart. I was never so scared in my life. I feel like the time I peed myself at school when I was six years old after they told me I couldn't use the girl's bathroom. I can't take it, Stu. I can't take it. I have do something 'bout this man.

STUART Have faith, girl.

SIMONE It's all I have left. Anyway, now that the Phantom has materialized, can we get him to show his face at the next UGLAAB meeting?

STUART He hates UGLAAB. Too aggressive, he says. He especially don't like hearing me talk about our efforts to repeal the buggery laws. He doesn't think we should bring attention to a law that's not even enforced.

SIMONE But he's so wrong. Because of that law they can't distribute condoms in jail. And that would save a lotta lives.

STUART That's what I try to tell him.

SIMONE Stu, don't take this the wrong way, but are you sure this is the man you want to be with?

STUART Other than that, he's wonderful.

SIMONE   Better you than me, honey. I'm going up. You know your way around. The guest room is...

STUART   All made up... I know.

SIMONE/STUART   (*Together.*) You never know when Prince Charming might come knocking. (*They high five.*)

SIMONE   Just so we're straight. You're not Prince Charming, ok? (*They laugh.* SIMONE *leaves.* STUART *sits back. He hears a noise outside and grabs cutlass before going to check. He opens the door.* GABRIEL *enters. They stare at each other in the shadowy area near the door.*)

GABRIEL   Thought I'd find you here. (*Notices cutlass.*) What's that for?

STUART   What're you doing here?

GABRIEL   I could ask you the same thing.

STUART   I live here.

GABRIEL   You live here? (*Notices the bruise on* STUART'S *face and goes to him.*) Oh my God! What happened to you?

STUART   Leave me alone.

GABRIEL   What happened?

STUART   What're you doing here, Gabriel?

GABRIEL   I went to your house.

STUART   You went to my house?

GABRIEL   Your father was very nasty. Threatened me. Will you please tell me what happened?

STUART   You went to my house?

GABRIEL Yes… What?

STUART I'm… shocked.

GABRIEL You left me no choice.

STUART I almost stayed in New York, you know.

GABRIEL You don't need New York.

STUART So you keep telling me.

GABRIEL Let's go home.

STUART Home?

GABRIEL Yes.

STUART Are you asking me to move in with you?

GABRIEL No… I meant…

STUART Oh, just for the night. And what happens tomorrow when your mother wants to come over? Which closet will you stash me in this time?

GABRIEL Come, we can talk about it in the car.

STUART I'm not going with you.

GABRIEL Be reasonable, Stu.

STUART You swallowed all that poison, remember? I'm left with nothing but being unreasonable. And you know what? I kinda like the taste of it. Like… ah…. Like champagne. You want a glass?

GABRIEL (*Walks up to* STUART *and drapes a hand over his shoulder. Begins to caresses his head, but* STUART *pushes him away and walks away.*) Come home with me. There's some very exciting news I want to share with you. Champagne's home on ice.

STUART   If champagne's all you're offering, Simone has the most expensive champagne here.

GABRIEL   You know what, Stu... I know what you're trying to do. I'm not going to let you antagonize me.

STUART   Good. Scamper back to your hole. Cockroach!

GABRIEL   Don't call me that!

STUART   Cockroach! (GABRIEL *become angry and pushes* STUART *violently.* STUART *slaps him.* GABRIEL *raises his fist to strike* STUART.) What? Go ahead. Tonight's the night for it.

GABRIEL   Don't you miss me?

STUART   That's so lame. (*After a beat,* GABRIEL *turns and slowly walks out.* STUART *puts champagne bottle to his mouth and drinks as lights fade.*)

ACT ONE

SCENE FIVE

Two weeks later. Late evening. Simone's Place. SOLACE *is sitting at the bar drinking.* STUART *is behind the bar. Occasionally, he busies himself moving cases and answering the phone.* MOSES *enters. He has a bulging shopping bag which he puts on the counter. He looks tired. He sits next to* SOLACE.

MOSES   Stu, gimme a beer, there. (*Looks over at* SOLACE.) How you doing, Solace?

SOLACE   Wuh in the bag?

MOSES   How you doing, Solace?

SOLACE   I doing good. Wuh in the bag?

MOSES   It en fuh you.

SOLACE   I still waan know wuh in it.

MOSES   Some spouge records fuh Simone.

SOLACE   And you had to carry me 'round the world to say that? (*Pause.*) You look like you ready fuh dead, boy.

MOSES   I en step out the workshop in days. This is nights now I en sleep. (STUART *brings beer.* MOSES *sips. Sighs.*)

SOLACE   I see that. I know you suffer with insomnia like you grandmother.

MOSES   Who tell you I suffer with insomnia?

SOLACE   Moses, I know more things 'bout you than you think.

MOSES   Like wuh so?

SOLACE   I know yuh lost yuh virginity down under the plum tree when yuh was fifteen to a woman old enough to be yuh mother. Madelene Jones, the hairdresser who was married to Lincoln Jones at the time. I know you went to jail for stealing a gun from the plantation when you was nineteen, but before that I know you do something else that you still feel shame 'bout to this day. Satisfied? (*Long pause.*) Don't ever challenge me, hear? I was a bird in another life... So wuh got you working so hard?

MOSES   Something new for a show in New York.

SOLACE   Oh, yeah. I hear yuh got a 'Merican woman now.

MOSES   (*Laughs. Takes another sip of beer, sighs even louder.*) You en gine stop spreading rumors, though?

SOLACE   Only if you give me what I want.

MOSES   You seen Pecong today?

SOLACE   No. And I can say I'm happier for it.

MOSES   He en that bad, yuh know.

SOLACE   You're right. He's worse.

MOSES   You don't understand Pecong.

SOLACE   Oh really... And you do? He ever tell you 'bout the night he foop Simone?

STUART   Solace...

SOLACE   Stay outta this, Stuart. (MOSES *looks at* SOLACE *then at* STUART *then back at* SOLACE.) Poor Moses. Look so shocked. Stu, I think Moses need something a little stiffer than that beer. (*Laughs.*) Do you know the reason he been getting on so burn is because he jealous?

MOSES   Jealous of wuh?

SOLACE   Of whom.

MOSES   Of whom?

SOLACE   Of you. Simone is in love with you. You must know that. (STUART *leaves to go stack chairs at back of club.*)

MOSES   Stop talking foolishness, Solace.

SOLACE   Don't play stupid to catch wise, Moses. You have to know that. You think you smart. That if you ignore the obvious it would go away. Well, in case the newsflash en get to you yet, it en only Simone one up here itching to drop their panties fuh you. How long I did trying to get you to notice me and you refuse to take me on.

MOSES   So, you're saying you in love with me, too?

SOLACE   Yes, Moses, I'm in love with you. (*Sarcastically, after no response from* MOSES.) You are truly an idiot savant when it comes to women.

MOSES   What you know 'bout love, Solace? I don't see you with a man no longer than three weeks.

SOLACE   I don't keep garbage 'til it stink. Cause you frighten fuh love, don't mean I am.

MOSES   Who say I frighten?

SOLACE   Then what is it, Moses? There en three women up here look better than me. You know how many men up here was trying to foop me since I was fifteen? You prefer somebody like Simone?

MOSES   You don't think it's time you stop running your mouth, though?

SOLACE   If you marry me I won't have time to do that. It would be too full of your man milk. (MOSES *laughs.*) You find that funny? (*Pokes* MOSES.) Why you think that was funny? (MOSES *pokes her back.* SOLACE *pokes him again. Harder this time.*) Why you think that's funny, man? (SOLACE *tries to slap him.* MOSES *grabs her arm. They wrestle.* MOSES *holds her tight to prevent her from striking him. They end up with* MOSES *behind* SOLACE *holding her around the waist.*) I know you want me, Moses. But you frighten. You know if you taste this you en going ever leave it. (MOSES *doesn't move.*) I want to breed for you, yuh know. I'm very fertile. I can even breed by osmosis. If you stay there two more minutes is a boy we having nine months from now. (MOSES *moves away quickly.*)

MOSES   How you getting on with Albert? He teaching you anything?

SOLACE   (*Follows* MOSES. *She's close to his face. Close enough to kiss.*) Are you going to let somebody else come along and take me, Moses?

MOSES   (*Finishes beer, gets up to leave.*) Stu! (STUART *returns from storage room.*) How much I got fuh you?

STUART   Three fifty.

MOSES   (*Puts money on counter. Starts off.*) I'm off to see the wizard, Solace.

SOLACE   Yuh off to see the wizard? Yuh brute! Go 'long. Why you don't beg he for a heart? Or soul. If you hear I getting married... (MOSES *exits.*)

STUART   Why you tell him that lie?

SOLACE   What lie?

STUART   That... About Simone and Pecong.

SOLACE   How you know it's a lie?

STUART   It's a lie. Not in a million years would Simone let Pecong touch her.

SOLACE   She's my competition. All's fair in love and war. Shakespeare said it. Good enough for me.

STUART   Shakespeare didn't say that.

SOLACE   How you know? You en drop out of school?

STUART   I have a B.A. in Spanish literature, I will have you know.

SOLACE   Spanish literature? You might is well did drop out of school. No wonder you working in here. Who said it then if it wasn't Shakespeare?

STUART   Well… A writer by the name of Frank Smedley. But Miguel de Cervantes first made the comparison between love and war in Don Quixote in sixteen oh four.

SOLACE   Smedley Smelly. Whatever. You making this up. Where Simone, man?

STUART   I hear you saying that there's something Moses real shame 'bout?

SOLACE   (*Long pause.*) Where Simone?

STUART   Tell me.

SOLACE   You too jipsee for a young man, yuh know.

STUART   Talk about the pot calling the kettle…

SOLACE   Don't say it.

STUART   Black.

SOLACE   I leffin in here. (*Gets up to leave.*)

STUART   You en pay for that beer in yuh hand.

SOLACE   Forget 'bout the beer… throw in a flask to go and I will tell you all about Moses.

STUART   Tell me first.

SOLACE   When Moses was a teenager… He… There was this man… (*Pause. Pulls $20 from pocket.*) Take out for the beer, and give me the flask.

STUART   No. You don't have to pay. Tell me 'bout Moses.

SOLACE   I change my mind.

(*We hear commotion from outside. Things crashing.*)

MOSES: (OFF STAGE)   Man, Pecong! No!

PECONG (OFF STAGE)   Let me go, Moses! Let me go!

SIMONE   (*Rushes in. She's out of breath.*) Oh my goodness! Moses and Pecong out there fighting! (STUART *and* SOLACE *rush out. Blackout.*)

ACT TWO

SCENE ONE

Three days later. Night. Simone's Place. The bar and tables are littered with empty beer bottles. Nina Simone's Do What You Gotta Do *wafts softly in the air.* STUART *enters hurriedly. He's dressed in pink shirt and white pants.* GABRIEL *follows in the same hurried manner. In his hand is a bottle of champagne. He's dressed sedately in brown slacks and brown shirt.*

STUART (*Takes a chair off the stack.*) I told you I didn't want to go to that stupid party.

GABRIEL (*Takes hold of chair before* STUART *can put it on the ground.*) It's a stupid party because it was something for me? Fifteen… twenty minutes we're there. I didn't even get a chance to open the damn champagne and you tell me you want to leave. Not even a goodbye to my friends. Now that was rude.

STUART You know why I wanted to leave?

SIMONE (*Offstage.*) Is that you down here, Stu?

STUART Yes, Simone. It's me.

SIMONE (*Appearing onstage. She's wrapped in a robe.*) Is everything okay?

STUART Yes, everything's fine.

SIMONE Hi Gabriel.

GABRIEL Hi Simone.

SIMONE I see where this one acquired his taste for champagne.

GABRIEL We were supposed to be celebrating tonight.

SIMONE   Really? What's the occasion?

GABRIEL   My promotion to assistant headmaster.

SIMONE   Congratulations.

GABRIEL   Thank you. I wish somebody else felt the same way.

STUART   What're you doing here? Thought you left for the Bahamas this evening.

SIMONE   Last minute change of plans. Leaving in the morning. (*Turns to go.*) Well, enjoy your champagne.

STUART   Saw Moses as we were driving up.

SIMONE   He just left.

STUART   Oh...

SIMONE   Nothing so promising. He just came by to bring me some more spouge records.

STUART   He hasn't been in since the fight. How is he?

GABRIEL   What fight?

STUART   I heard that...

SIMONE   I really don't know how he is. He won't talk about it. (SIMONE *turns to go.*)

GABRIEL   Can I ask you something? (SIMONE *stops.*) Your real name is Percival Springer, isn't it? And Sir Franklyn Springer is your uncle.

SIMONE   I'm Lady Simone.

GABRIEL   I don't get it, though.

SIMONE   Get what?

GABRIEL You. Here. Like... Acting like you're an ordinary...

SIMONE Ordinary? Where do you see ordinary?

GABRIEL Pretending you're...

SIMONE I don't need to pretend.

GABRIEL Stuart thinks he can be like you. All out in the open. But he's naïve.

STUART Because I don't want to live like a cockroach, I'm naïve?

GABRIEL Explain to him.

SIMONE Explain what?

GABRIEL That he can't get away with the things that you can get away with.

SIMONE What is it that I get away with?

GABRIEL I know a little more about this country than you think. I know about that guy who attacked you a few years ago. He's still regretting it to this day. If that was anybody else... If that was me or Stuart...

SIMONE I don't care to have this discussion with you. Good night. (SIMONE *leaves.*)

STUART That wasn't nice.

GABRIEL Must be nice being her, though.

STUART What do you have against Simone?

GABRIEL (*Sarcastically.*) You think I care about having the privilege to flout society? It must take great courage to wear make-up knowing full well there'd be no ramifications. That nobody will touch you.

STUART   Simone is being herself. Stop hating. And yes, that takes courage. Even if you come from privilege. She's unapologetic. You know, in some cultures people like Simone are thought to have both the spirit of a man and the spirit of a woman. She embraces the duality. And since everything that exists is thought to come from the spirit, two-spirit people, like Simone, are then doubly blessed. And they're honored instead of persecuted.

GABRIEL   Oh, please! Your mysticism is lost on me, you know that. Some of us have to be careful who we expose our lives too. For some of us, there're consequences.

STUART   Choices, Gabriel. Choices. That's what it's about.

GABRIEL   Stop it, will you! Just stop it! I'm sick of your selfishness, Stu. See my side for a change. Can you do that? Can you squeeze a little bit of compassion out of that tiny world you live in? For goodness sake! I have a life to live here.

STUART   And I don't?

GABRIEL   I teach at a very important school. I look after people. People depend on me. My mother. My grandmother. They're old-fashioned. And very religious.

STUART   A bunch of foolish hypocrites.

GABRIEL   Don't talk about my family like that.

STUART   Well, they are. Your aunt...Ah... the one who's married to a judge. Didn't you tell me she came home and caught him in bed with her niece? Did she leave him? No.

GABRIEL   I'm not telling you anything else about my family... You know what my mother told me when I was fourteen. She looked me dead in the face and said. 'If I find out you's a buller I will kill you.'

STUART   All mothers say that when their sons are fourteen.

GABRIEL   Really? Did yours?

STUART   Mine told me she would cut off my doggie and feed it to the pig.

GABRIEL   *(Laughs.)* You're lying!

STUART   Kid you not.

GABRIEL   I think I'm still traumatized me.

STUART   You're letting yourself be a victim.

GABRIEL   Easy for you to talk. This is still Barbados! You could pick up your ass and fly to New York if things don't go your way. I can't. *(Long pause.)* Say we do this. What's going to happen the next time I pass the priest in the church vestibule? Is he going to shake my hand and say: 'How's your boyfriend?' Or is he going to whisper that I'm not welcome in his church after he condemns me to hell.

STUART   Because you fell in love?

GABRIEL   Because I fell from grace.

STUART   For daring to live with the one you love?

GABRIEL   Oh, how clever. Not the *one*, Stuart. The *man*. Let's get it straight. It's bad enough that whenever he preaches the sins of homosexuality, and starts quoting Leviticus and Romans, he stares directly at me.

STUART   That's because he's got the hots for you.

GABRIEL   You're hopeless.

STUART   Tell him about all the stuff you tell me? About David and Jonathon being lovers.

GABRIEL   I never said they were lovers.

STUART   Yes, you did. You said that... I forgot now. Something David said to Jonathon about his love surpassing the love of women.

GABRIEL   In Samuel. "David laments thy love to me was wonderful, surpassing the love of women."

STUART   What is that, huh? What is that if not two men loving each other. Right there in the great book. Why don't you tell the preacher about that?

GABRIEL   Nothing he hasn't heard before. And he would skilfully challenge that interpretation.

STUART   You really think your mother don't know that you're gay?

GABRIEL   My mother makes a very compelling ostrich. As long as I don't confirm it, it's not true. Why do we need to live together to prove we love each other?

STUART   This isn't about proving love. You think this is about proving love? We're past that stage. This is about acceptance. About family. I want to wake up in the morning... every morning and make breakfast for you. I want to be there when you come home from work.

GABRIEL   What? With your little apron on?

STUART   (*Laughing.*) White apron, if you please. And no underwear.

GABRIEL   I've been making my own breakfast for fifteen years without any trouble. My goodness! Boy, you want to kill me? Why couldn't I've fallen in love with a normal Bajan girl who finds pleasure in secrets. Whose eyes embrace the dark.

STUART   Are you really happy this way?

GABRIEL   It is what it is, Stu. We have to wear the mask to survive. We don't all have Simone's pedigree. And even she's wearing a mask. Hiding out among the... the plebs.

STUART   Leave Simone out of this.

GABRIEL   She's the one filling up your head with all this stuff. All the obeah nonsense. Your rituals to the ancestors and all that foolishness.

STUART   Do I make fun of your religion?

GABRIEL   I'm sorry. Let's go home, Stu.

STUART   Home? Is that our home?... I didn't think so. (*Long pause.*) You know why I don't like those parties? Why I want to leave as soon as I get there? I feel more claustrophobic there than anywhere else. It's the only parties we get to go to together. I feel like I'm at some secret society convention. The Rosicrucians or something.

GABRIEL   Aren't you part of one? What about those ceremonies Simone take you to, with your... whatever orishas and spirits?

STUART   Stop right now! Stop! Not another word because without them I wouldn't be able to live in this place.

GABRIEL   And without my friends...

STUART   Are they really your friends? Ah? You mean those big important doctors and lawyers and judges who keep trying to slip me their phone number? Those friends? With all that money and position and still living like cockroaches. Those friends?

GABRIEL   To hell with you, Stu. You want to see a gay-pride parade through my house and in my backyard, but I can't do it. It may not be New York, but it ain't as bad as some other places.

STUART   I want our relationship to be real.

GABRIEL   Because I prefer to keep it hidden from prying eyes does-n't mean it's not real. What can be more real than how I feel when I hear your voice? What can be more real that the empti-ness I have when you leave my house and I want to run after you and bring you back... Let's face it. Secrets are the fabric of society, Stu. Of any society, but especially ours.

STUART   When secrets start to strangle you, it's time...

GABRIEL   (*Interrupting him.*) We used to have a neighbor when I lived in Darryls Road. A butcher. Sloppy guy, but very nice. Used to bring meat for us every weekend. Beef. Mutton. Pork. Sometimes more than we needed. After he died we dis-covered that he'd left my sister a piece of land. My sister was confused. Why would this man leave her land? He had a wife. And children. Finally, my mother confessed. The butcher was my sister's father. Almost sent my sister crazy. All this time she believed her father had gone to England when she was a baby and never came back. That was her story. Was a myth, but it was her story. A narrative she understood and had grown accustomed to. She couldn't see without her mask. We have to find a story we can live with.

STUART   No, you're letting them create our story for their amuse-ment... I had another visitation.

GABRIEL   Oh Christ, Stu. Don't start with your mumbo-jumbo again. How's he getting along with the ancestors?

STUART   I told you not to do that.

GABRIEL   Oh, you can make fun of my living family, but I can't make fun of your dead ones?

STUART   I felt his spirit, Gabe. When he died I felt it. As if his spir-it was entering my body. I woke up in the middle of the night crying. He had a good heart. But he was a troubled, troubled man. He pretended he was somebody he was not. And when he couldn't hide any longer when he was forced to face who he was inside, it didn't turn out good. Made him run from Barbados. He never got over it. Made him so bitter. And angry. And I think it also made him foolhardy and reckless. And you know what that did.

GABRIEL You never told me the full story. What happened here to make him run away?

STUART   Doesn't matter now. The point is, he lived a life filled with bitterness and regret. I don't want to hide who I am. I can't.

GABRIEL Jesus, Stu! You don't think I wish it was different? Ah? You don't think I wish… It kills me, you know… It kills me… Having to… Having to… There's nothing I can do, Stu. There's nothing I can do. You know why I have my mother visit me? I hate going back there. To that village. That backward… That… I was there a few weeks ago. Had to go. My sister's… My niece… her birthday party. Had to go. And, I decided to take a walk to watch a football match on the pitch behind my mother's house. As I passed a group of fellas playing dominoes, I heard one sing out: "Looka bulling Gabriel. All them fuckers full of AIDS." I didn't look back. I didn't stop. I circled the field and went back and went back and got in my car and drove home. Didn't even say goodbye to my mother.

STUART   I woulda turn round and slap he hard as shite.

GABRIEL That's how they see us, Stu.

STUART   Their problem.

GABRIEL Ours too. If we want to live here. We're nasty bullers. Everybody makes fun of us. People in the street. Comedians. When's the last time you seen a comedy play in Barbados that didn't make fun of us? No amount of PSAs, or educational literature about AIDS seem to change how they think.

STUART   If we don't fight back, we will always be defined by what they say.

GABRIEL You never want to see the world as it is.

STUART   Living the life we deserve. Not how we're expected to live. Not hiding. In the shadows. Not so they can feel comfortable. We're no different. No better. No worse. Our lives, Gabriel, are real. Drag their heads out of the fucking sand. Love isn't something to be ashamed of. If we can't live together here, then let's go somewhere else. Leave 'bout here.

GABRIEL I'm not leaving Barbados.

STUART   (*Turns. Nina Simone's* Do What You Gotta Do *rises*) Then I may as well go back to New York.

GABRIEL Stu… I've built a foundation here. For us.

STUART   It's sand, Gabriel. Sand.

GABRIEL A lot of people here… A lot of important people. They have time for me.

STUART   I see what's important to you. After the opening of Simone's new show I'm gone. (GABRIEL *walks over and takes his bottle of champagne from the bar and walks away.*) You will miss me. Mark my word. And you will hate yourself. (GABRIEL *disappears. Lights fade to black.*)

ACT TWO

SCENE TWO

A week later. Late evening. Simone's Place. MOSES *seated at the bar nursing a beer. His hand is bandaged. Nina Simone's* I Need Some Sugar in My Bowl is playing. STUART *enters carrying a case of beer..*

STUART   She said you called her two days ago. (STUART *traverses to the storage area. Returns with another case of beer*) She was so pumped about it... She wanted to skip the show and take the next flight home.

MOSES   Because I called her?

STUART   How did you know where she was staying?

MOSES   I didn't. Called her cell to tell her this art magazine in New York called me. Somehow they got hold of that thing she wrote in the newsletter and wanted to reprint.

STUART   That's awesome!

MOSES   (MOSES *points to empty beer bottle.* STUART *brings beer.*) How's rehearsals for the new show coming?

STUART   She won't let nobody watch.

MOSES   Not even you?

STUART   I sneaked a peek, but I'm not supposed to say.

MOSES   The secret's out. The backup singers telling everybody. People excited. I hear Joel Grant and his wife talking 'bout practicing their Spouge moves.

STUART   She really into the spouge now, fuh truth. I hear she singing 'Come here to drink milk' the other day...

MOSES   (*Sings.*)
Come here to drink milk
Or you come here fuh count cow
(STUART *joins in the singing.*)
Come here to drink milk
Or you come here fuh count cow
When yuh go to Rome
yuh gotta do like the Romans do
If yuh see them laugh
That you must also do
(*Laughing, they high-five.*)

STUART   Can I ask you something?

MOSES   Leave it alone.

STUART   Do you think… Would he have…

MOSES   Shite! I said leave it alone, man! (*Long pause.*) Sorry.

STUART   My fault. I shouldn't…

MOSES   I couldn't stand by while he incited them fellas he was drinking with to hurt Simone. I had to remind him that it was Simone who helped him get the bank loan to buy that boat he got. He didn't like that and we scuffled.

STUART   You know I gay, right?

MOSES   (*Teasing.*) Are you really?

STUART   You serious? (MOSES *laughs.* STUART *tosses a bottle cap at him.*) Moses, the cursing we does get, hear. The name calling. The bad looks.

MOSES   You ever get frighten?

STUART   Sometimes. You try hard not to show it. I know they're just doing what society gives them permission to do. It's like… You feel like you're in a prison. Partly a psychological prison of your own making, so it's confusing. You have a little bit of freedom as long as you don't piss off the guards. They're watching you. Taunting you. Laughing. Hoping you make a mistake. It's the menace, you know what I mean. Because you have to learn to take it. You have to try not to snap... I had an uncle...

MOSES   Yeah. I know.

STUART   You know what?

MOSES   Your uncle... He was a straight guy. Not straight in that way. You know. Straight as in honest. He was very honest about... Shocked me at first.

STUART   You were...

MOSES   Of course not... Just... He gave me books, you know. Books on art and stuff like that. When I was starting out. African art and stuff. Encouraged me to study art history. I liked him. Very smart fella. Then... (*Long pause.*) One day he said something to me. And I told my friends what he said. It was foolish. They made me feel shame.

STUART   What did he say to you?

MOSES   That he loved me.

STUART   And you told your friends that?

MOSES   Yes. They... They got me to set up a date.

STUART   Oh no, Moses. No. (*Long pause.*)

MOSES   Yeah. Was... He held my hand. That was the signal. They... Was an ambush.

STUART   I can't... Don't... (SOLACE *enters singing:* I put a Spell on You. *She's dressed chic. Nicely fitted dress. Her hair is done. She's wearing heels.*)

SOLACE   Simone reach yet? (*Long pause.*) Wuh happen? Both ah wunna catch a stroke? Stuart, you okay?

STUART   Yes… Yes… I'm fine.

SOLACE   You sure?

STUART   (*Pouring a large drink. He snaps back his head and drains the glass.*) Yes. I'm good… And you. I can tell… You… You look bliss, baby.

SOLACE   Thank you, Stuart… Moses?

MOSES   Bliss…Yeah… Bliss is the right choice.

SOLACE   That's Stu's word, Moses. Find your own damn word. Even when you offer me a compliment it's stale. A woman can't win with you, boy.

MOSES   What's the occasion?

SOLACE   I need an occasion to dress nice? (MOSES *shrugs.*) Simone upstairs?

STUART   She en reach yet.

SOLACE   I en just ask you that? Christmas, man! I thought she was coming back today.

STUART   She stop off to see her aunt first. She soon here.

MOSES   Wuh you drinking, Solace?

SOLACE   You offering me a drink, Moses?

MOSES   Yes, I am. And you look beautiful. Amazing actually.

SOLACE   I'll drink to that. Johnny Walker. Black. (STUART *pours whisky.* MOSES *attempts to pay for the drink but* SOLACE *stops him. She puts 20 dollars down on the bar.*) I appreciate the offer. But, I'm paying for my own drinks. Thanks for the compliment, though. (MOSES *puts his money away in silence.*) I surprise to see you here.

MOSES   Me? Why?

SOLACE   I figured… I figured you'd be at the airport.

MOSES   Fuh what?

SOLACE   I figured… I figured you'd be at the airport.

MOSES   For what?

SOLACE   Yuh think I en know 'bout the phone call to the Bahamas? Take care yuh don't end up just like Pecong. Where he is, though? I hear the two of wunna 'gree back already.

MOSES   Out on his boat.

SOLACE   Hope he drown out there. He ass belong in jail. (PECONG *enters as* SOLACE *is finishing her sentence.*)

PECONG   Who that belong in jail? (SOLACE *crosses quickly to* PECONG *and slaps him in the face.* PECONG *is too stunned to do anything.* MOSES *rushes over to separate them.*)

SOLACE   You en got nuh shame, though? You got the nerve to come back in here?

STUART   He en welcome in here.

MOSES   Stu, you know Simone wouldn't do this.

STUART   Simone isn't here right now.

PECONG   I get a call from Simone not long ago. Told me to meet she here.

STUART   I don't belive you.

MOSES   Wuh you drinking, Pecong?

STUART   I en serving he.

SOLACE   That's right, Stuart. Don't serve he.

MOSES   Wunna give the man a break, nuh.

SOLACE   The way he break you hand? Definitely.

MOSES   If Simone can forgive him, then that should be good enough for anybody in here.

STUART   Not fuh me.

SOLACE   Simone think she's Gandhi, but I don't look good in pajamas.

MOSES   I know you don't like Pecong, but…

SOLACE   Is time Pecong face his self otherwise he gine do something even worse that what you do, Moses.

MOSES   We all make mistakes. It ain't like you's a saint yuh know, Solace.

SOLACE   I en nuh saint, but at least I know who I is. Ask Pecong who he is.

MOSES   Leave the man alone, alright? Just leave him alone. Wuh you drinking, man?

PECONG   Guinness.

MOSES   You heard the man, Stu. (STUART *does not move.*)

SOLACE   I leaving in here so. In fact, I came in here to tell you all goodbye. The next time you see me, if you do, I will be wearing a wedding ring.

STUART You serious? (SOLACE *displays engagement ring.*) That's awesome, sweetie. Congratulations!

SOLACE As Shakespeare said: If Mohammad can't come to the mountain, the mountain must go to Mohammad.

STUART I don't think Shakespeare said that.

SOLACE Well, he shoulda said it.

MOSES Who's the lucky man?

SOLACE Wouldn't you like to know. I may not have a lot of education, but I could out talk the Devil. I funny. I sincere. And hardworking. And I'm a good mother. And I good as shite in bed. There's somebody who admire these qualities even if you don't. You gine miss me, Moses. Ah gone. (SOLACE *leaves.*)

PECONG That woman crazy, hear.

MOSES Stu, where the man Guinness?

STUART I en serving he. Why he got to come here?

SIMONE (*Entering. She's dressed exquisitely in an orange pants suit.*) Because there's only one Simone's Place.

STUART Simone! (STUART *rushes over to* SIMONE. *Hugs her.*)

MOSES Simone. How you, girl?

SIMONE I'll be much better if you come and give me a hug, Moses King. (MOSES *goes over, hugs* SIMONE.) You just made me feel like I was sixteen again. Pecong. It's good to see you.

PECONG I so sorry, Simone

SIMONE You look sorry in that ugly shirt. Come and give me a hug, nuh. (PECONG *slowly treads over to* SIMONE. *They hug.*) How you doing? (PECONG *remains silent.*) I would like to speak to Pecong alone, please.

STUART   You sure?

SIMONE   Yes, I'm sure Stuart Fowler. (STUART *and* MOSES *leave.* SIMONE *sits slowly.*) You alright? (PECONG *doesn't respond.*) I was lying on the beach and that's when it hit me. Did you go get the test?

PECONG   No.

SIMONE   Then what's going on?

PECONG   I need... I need money.

SIMONE   You need money? (PECONG *nods.*) How much?

PECONG   A lot.

SIMONE   What for?

PECONG   Don't ask me what for.

SIMONE   I'm sorry then...

PECONG   What you mean sorry? This is your fault. (*Advancing menacingly.*) You destroyed my life.

SIMONE   Just relax, okay.

PECONG   (*Fist balled.*) Don't fucking tell me relax.

SIMONE   I'm not afraid of you, Pecong.

PECONG   I shouldn'ta listen to you.

SIMONE   Whatever it is you're talking about...

PECONG   You know what I'm talking about. That night we were here... alone. Talking.

SIMONE   What about it?

PECONG   I told you some things... That... That I was feeling. Things that... About a certain fella from St Philip that I took out on the boat. And you told me...

SIMONE   To follow your heart...

PECONG   Why did you have to tell me to do that for?

SIMONE   What should I've told you? To go to church? To pray and hope the feeling go away? I would've been a hypocrite.

PECONG   Follow my heart... That is bare shite.

SIMONE   Thought you were happy with your decision. You enjoyed being with him. You told me that you realized being with a woman wasn't what you really wanted.

PECONG   Maybe it's what a man like me should want.

SIMONE   Then go back to the woman. What do you want from me?

PECONG   He wants money.

SIMONE   Who... The fella? Why?

PECONG   Why you think?

SIMONE   How much?

PECONG   Five thousand.

SIMONE   Don't pay him a penny. Let him talk.

PECONG   I'm a fucking fisherman. I en one your bulling friends.

SIMONE   Actually, you are.

PECONG   (PECONG *charges.* SIMONE *pushes him back forcefully and takes a pugnacious posture.* PECONG *stops.*) I's a real man, alright. I en like you.

SIMONE   Honey, I'm not even like me. There's only one star in the firmament of Lady Simone. Why do you care what he says. Unless he's got pictures then...

PECONG   You understand now?

SIMONE   You let him take pictures, Pecong?

PECONG   I was drunk. I was... I trusted him.

SIMONE   You want me to give you the money, is that what this is about?

PECONG   You have it. I know you have it.

SIMONE   What I have is not your business.

PECONG   *(Pushing Simone.)* I need that money.

SIMONE   And I said no. I can help you if you want, but I'm not giving you that money.

PECONG   *(Grabs Simone's neck.)* You think everybody is you, ah? Everybody ain't you.

SIMONE   Let me go, Pecong.

PECONG   You're going to give me that money. *(Pecong has Simone pushed up against the bar. Simone reaches around and finds a scissors. She presses it against Pecong's jugular.)*

SIMONE   Get up off me! *(Pecong releases Simone and backs away.)* Who the fuck do you think you're messing with? If you want to choke somebody, why don't you go and choke him? You can fix this by being honest with yourself. He can't hurt you if you're honest. You claim you're a real man, but you don't have any balls. Get a set of balls, Pecong. I could give you mine because I don't need them. But you probably won't know what to do with them.

PECONG   Everybody can't be free like you, Simone.

SIMONE   Sometimes trying to fit in is harder than to be free, *(Takes pen and paper from behind bar.)* Write this guy's name and address. I know a couple of Israeli ex-soldiers who do private security for a very wealthy Russian family on the island. They'll make him an offer he can't refuse.

PECONG   What kind of offer?

SIMONE   You don't want to know. Trust me.

PECONG   I feel like jumping in the sea.

SIMONE   Great idea. Nothing like a sea bath to cleanse away bad spirits.

PECONG   I don't mean to bathe.

SIMONE   Please! What else? You born with gills. *(Touches* PECONG'S *neck.)* Can't drown even if you tried.

PECONG   *(Writes the name on the paper.)* I wish I wasn't this way. That I could change myself. Stop myself from wanting to do that nastiness. I can't even tell my best friend. How can a man like me live this life? I was able to fight this thing for so long... so long. And now I don't know who I am. Tell the God's truth... I shame of the things... the things I want to do. I gotta find a way to change back. *(Pecong turns and looks at Simone for a long time. Nina Simone's* Just Like Tom Thumb's Blues *swells. Pecong slowly walks away.)*

SIMONE   Pecong (PECONG *stops.)* At least tell your best friend. *(*PECONG *leaves.* SIMONE *picks up paper Pecong left behind. Exists as lights fade)*

ACT TWO

SCENE THREE

A week later. Late evening. Simone's Place. SIMONE *directing her dancers. She isn't happy with the way rehearsals are going and stops the music.* MOSES, *with his hand still bandaged enters and stands off watching.*

SIMONE   Why're you all half-stepping in my rehearsal? Please take your Geritol before you come here, old ladies. Go home. Rehearsals over for the day. Be back here tomorrow at five. And be ready to dance. No more snoozing on the beat. (*The dancers gather their equipment and leave.*)

MOSES   Looks like I just missed getting a sneak peek.

SIMONE   Hi Moses. Be here Saturday night and you sneak all the peeks you want. If you're a good boy I may even let you into my dressing room. (MOSES *laughs.*) How's that hand?

MOSES   Almost there.

SIMONE   I'm glad. You sound like your old self. Drink?

MOSES   Stout... Stu told me you wanted to see me.

SIMONE   (*Goes to bar.*) A stout? Somebody doing hard work.

MOSES   I always working hard.

SIMONE   I bet. (*Returns with a Guinness and a beer. She hands stout to Moses.*) Haven't seen you in here much since I had that talk with Pecong.

MOSES   Been real busy.

SIMONE   I still can't believe what you did for me. Defending my honor against your best friend.

MOSES   It wasn't nothing.

SIMONE   Can a girl have her fantasy? (*Pause.*) Before I forget. Thank your grandmother for sending me that breadfruit cou cou yesterday. It was just what I was craving.

MOSES   No problem.

SIMONE   I bet it's you tell her to send it... I knew it. You're so good to me, Moses.

MOSES   It's nothing.

SIMONE   What motivated you do it? Risk yourself to protect me? You could easily have walked away. (*Moses doesn't respond.*) OK. If that's what you want... I'll let you have your secret. You know, in this country we value secrets like money. Secrets and brightness. The brighter you are, the more secrets you get to keep. The name my parents gave me is Percival Springer... I have an uncle who is a knight of St. Andrew. Sir Franklyn Springer.

MOSES   Oh wow! Sir Franklyn? You family's... ah...

SIMONE   A family of lawyers. I actually have a law degree, too. There was a time when I actually thought of being a lawyer. Can you imagine me in court? What a spectacle that would've been. Never practiced. My mother still haven't forgiven me. When my uncle was being knighted many in the family didn't want me to come. But he insisted on me coming. Simone never hid from me, so she's coming, he told them. I wore a lime green suit and stole the show. Me and my uncle still laugh about it. Why'm I telling you this? When I was relaxing on the beach in the Bahamas I had time to think about what you did for me. And I felt it's time you know the way I feel about you.

MOSES   What you trying to say, Simone?

SIMONE   How do you see me, Moses? Do you think I'm a freak?

MOSES   How do I see you? I don't know. How you mean?

SIMONE   In your eyes. A man? Woman? None of the above. (MOSES *fidgets, but doesn't answer.*) No sexual identity? I'm having my operation in Miami in six months. When I fully become a woman, could you love me? (MOSES *doesn't answer.*) So many men does be trying to talk to me, Moses. Single. Married. Gay. Bisexual. Even some women. I don't even know what that's about. Well, I think I do. Women are strange like that. Half the time it isn't me they're interested in. I know that. It's the image. The idea. The curiosity. They don't see me as a man nor a woman. I'm a freak in most people's eyes. And that hurts, Moses. More than anybody knows... I've been threatened... shot at... and beaten once. But this society can't do nothing to me that the ancestors haven't prepared me for. I'm not afraid. You know what scares me, Moses? My own heart. (*Long pause.*) I've always wanted to dance with you, did you know that?

MOSES   Didn't know that.

SIMONE   I have. And I was thinking... I was thinking what if I was to die and not get to dance with you? I'd go to greet the ancestors and they'd tell me: "We can't allow you to join us. We have to send your spirit back. You didn't dance with Moses." I've never had the courage to come out and tell you. The fear that you would reject me kept me tongue-tied. It drives me crazy, Moses. It drives me crazy that I love you and couldn't say it until now.

MOSES   That en you talking.

SIMONE   I love you, Moses.

MOSES   Don't say that. Don't fucking say that!

SIMONE   I know exactly when it happened, too... I had a friend visiting from California. I took them to the museum. And there I saw your three life-size Monkeys for the first time. You know, those ones you did with paintings on them depicting three births. The first birth into slavery in Barbados. The first birth after abolition. And the first birth after independence. It was transformative. I felt your soul. I know it sounds crazy. But I felt... I felt your spirit. The pain. The joy. Because only somebody searching their soul... who felt the past deep in their soul could've conceived that idea. And then to use Monkeys, something so quintessentially Bajan, as your palette.

MOSES   Tell me about you and Pecong.

SIMONE   Pecong?

MOSES   We had a talk...

SIMONE   Aaah!

MOSES   You had sex with him?

SIMONE   He told you that?

MOSES   Was that love?

SIMONE   Did Pecong tell you that?

PECONG   What happened the night the two of you were here alone drinking 'til morning? He said... He said that night changed his life.

SIMONE   I was lonely. I guess he was too. He confided in me. Things he had never told anybody. Not even you. That was it. Maybe it changed his life. Only time will tell. Why're you try-ing to hide behind Pecong? You know full well I would never sleep with Pecong. *(Pause.)* What do you want, Moses? Ah? You float around like this rare butterfly. Not connected to any-thing. How did you get this way?

MOSES   Don't get it twisted, Simone. Because I come in here and talk to you. Because I'm nice to you, don't mean nothing.

SIMONE   Is that right?

MOSES   And don't ever say you love me again.

SIMONE   I love you, Moses. I love you. What're you going to do?

MOSES   God damn you! Why can't we just be friends?

SIMONE   My heart can't keep. It's too fragile. (*Long pause.*) Dance with me, Moses.

MOSES   Why do you have to mess things up? Why? Why you got to go and mess things up? Why you had to go and talk to me like that? Like him. Just like him. We coulda been good friends. Told him not to say those fucking things. Told him... And my friends... they told me to play along... And then I couldn't stop them doing what they did. I couldn't...

SIMONE   Those boys not only broke Morton's foot... Maybe they broke your soul, too. It's time you heal, Moses.

MOSES   He trusted me.

SIMONE   I trust you.

MOSES   Why?

SIMONE   You're not the same person.

MOSES   I hear his screams sometimes. In my dreams. Murder! Murder! Murder! And I never told him... Never told him I'm sorry.

SIMONE   He already forgave you.

MOSES   How you know that?

SIMONE   I'm in touch with the ancestors. He visited Stu on his passage.

MOSES   (*After a long pause,* MOSES *walks up to* SIMONE *and takes her hand.*) You still want to dance with me?

SIMONE   Is that the way you ask a lady to dance, Moses King?

MOSES   May I have the pleasure of this dance, Lady Simone?

SIMONE   With pleasure, Mr. King. (*Fans herself.*) Wait, let me savor the moment. (*They dance as* SIMONE *sings ballad.*)
I'm coming home
Back home to you
And I know now for sure
that my wandering days are through
I've looked around
Most every place
And all I that I ever see is your lovely face.

MOSES   (*Separating from* SIMONE *who stops singing.*) Thank you, Simone.

SIMONE   I'm not going to give up, you know. Six months. (MOSES *exits.* SIMONE *gathers her gear.* STUART *rushes on. He's out of breath.*)

STUART   Simone! Simone!

SIMONE   What's the matter, Sugar?

STUART   I'm sorry, I just couldn't wait. (*He thrusts a key in front of* SIMONE'S *face.*) Look!

SIMONE   Oh my goodness! Is that what I think it is?

STUART   (*Jumping around wildly. He hugs* SIMONE.) Yes! Yes! Yes! He presented it to me all wrapped in a bow and everything. So romantic.

SIMONE   I'm so happy for you, darling. I love happy endings. I'm going upstairs to cry.

STUART   I'm so sorry. Here I am babbling on...

SIMONE   Don't stop. You have a reason to babble. I might never tell another soul I love them, but I'll live. The show will go on.

STUART   Can I do anything?

SIMONE   (*starts off.*) You came here to celebrate, didn't you? Go ahead.

STUART   Ah... Can I... Would you mind...

SIMONE   (*Offstage.*) Drink 'em all if you can. You earned it. (*Lights fade. The transition music here should be Spouge.*)

EPILOGUE

A few days later. Late evening. Simone's Place. An aura of pageantry, festivity and celebration. African masks and colorfully painted banners hang from the ceiling. Simone's dancers, colorfully costumed, dance onstage to It Was Written Down, *made popular in Barbados by the Draytons Two. They're carrying a long chord of yellow mini lights which they lay on the floor in a circle. Then* SIMONE *makes a grand entrance. She is wearing a shimmering gold dress, her hair done up in a bun. The music stops as she walks down stage, mic in hand, and stands in the middle of the circle of lights.*

SIMONE   My friends... My goodness! I see we've got a packed house tonight. Thank you all for coming. Welcome to Simone's Place. Welcome. I've been in love with Nina Simone ever since my aunt introduced me to her music when I was ten years old. Her voice, her spirit, her courage, her fearlessness, set me on the course I am on today. To be free. To live my life as a woman. Nina sang a song: Time They Are a Changin'. And she is so right about that. Tonight, we have a great show for you. One of my friends reminded me that Miss Simone spent some time in Barbados. From all reports she unleashed a whirlwind of passion on this island when she was here. And so, on the advice of my friend, I decided to reinvent my show. Nina sang Jazz, Gospel, Blues, Folk, Soul, R and B, and even Pop, so how would Miss Simone have interpreted our spouge? How would she've put her revolutionary mind to this new beat of a fledgling nation. But, before I give my impression of her spougeness, I want to acknowledge some very important people in the audience tonight. My good friend Pecong. Live free! My dear friend Moses. You continue to inspire not just me, but other artists who've experienced your work. Thank you. A special congratulations and thank you to the fiercest woman I know. Solace Mangrove. She's getting married soon. I love you, girl. And thank you for choosing to hold your wedding right here in Simone's Place.

(*Music. Dancers move downstage.* SIMONE *begins to sings* It Was Written Down, *in a jazzy spouge beat.* SIMONE *and dancers peform this song until lights fade.*)